rottweiler

understanding and
caring for your dog

Written by
Julie Johnson

rottweiler

understanding and
caring for your dog

Written by
Julie Johnson

Pet Book Publishing Company

St. Martin's Farm, Zeals, Warminster, BA12 6NZ, United Kingdom

Printed and bound in South Korea.

All rights reserved. No part of this work may be reproduced, in any form or by any means, electronic or mechanical, including photocopying, recording or by any information storage and retrieval system, without the prior written permission of the publisher.

Copyright © Pet Book Publishing Company 2012

Every reasonable care has been taken in the compilation of this publication. The Publisher and Author cannot accept liability for any loss, damage, injury or death resulting from the keeping of Rottweilers by user(s) of this publication, or from the use of any materials, equipment, methods or information recommended in this publication or from any errors or omissions that may be found in the text of this publication or that may occur at a future date, except as expressly provided by law.

The 'he' pronoun is used throughout this book instead of the rather impersonal 'it', however no gender bias is intended.

ISBN: 978-1-906305-62-8
ISBN: 1-906305-62-5

Acknowledgements

The author would like to thank the following: Jo Welch and Jane Chambers, who very kindly proof-read the book for me, and also John, my husband, who was great at helping and supporting me and pushing me to get the book done!

The publishers would like to thank the following for help with photography: Jenny Banham (Tallyman), Julia Williams (Bolia), Di McCann (Parvenue), Glynn Mulhall (Magglynn), Pam Rust with Barney, Andy Bashford with Zola and Rossie, Bethany and Katy Green with Tia and Kitty, John and Julie Johnson, and Lone Sveum Bertelsen.

Contents

Introducing the Rottweiler

Noble, powerful, impressive to look at, the Rottweiler is a breed like no other. He has strong guarding instincts but he is loyal and loving to his family, and is always eager to please.

This is a dog that loves to work; he is highly intelligent and therefore mental stimulation is essential. Among family and friends, he is laid back and likes nothing better than to make everyone laugh by playing the clown. This is not a breed for the faint-hearted, but if you have time to spend with your Rottweiler, socializing him and training him, he will be an outstanding family companion. The Rottweiler's behavior is self-assured, steady and fearless.

The feature that attracts me most about this breed is the loyalty Rottweilers show to their family, and the undying love they are capable of giving. I am also

drawn to their somewhat clownish nature – not a day goes by when I do not laugh at the antics of any one of my own four Rottweilers.

Family companion

If you are thinking of getting one of these magnificent creatures, or have already owned one, be prepared to be hooked for life. Many people who start out owning one dog will end up being a multi-Rottweiler household.

This is a relatively easy breed to care for. His smart short coat needs minimal grooming, and, as long as care is taken during the vulnerable growing stage, he thrives on a routine of regular, varied exercise. With good management – and good luck – most Rottweilers will live past the age of ten.

Rottweilers get on well with other dogs, and adapt to living with other, smaller breeds. In most cases, a mixed pair – male and female – will get on best, but for this to work successfully both dogs should be neutered. Same sex pairs have a tendency to squabble, and this can lead to serious problems if it is not nipped in the bud.

A Rottweiler will live happily alongside cats, rabbits, guinea pigs, horses and just about any other animal as long as he has been correctly socialized with

A Rottweiler will happily live with other dogs – big or small.

these from a young age and taught not to chase them. However, it must be remembered that all dogs are predators, and, if left unsupervised, your Rottweiler may chase a small animal and unintentionally harm it.

The Rottweiler sees himself as family protector; he will be tolerant of children, and may bond closely with them if mutual respect is established at an early stage. Bear in mind that a cuddly Rottweiler puppy will grow into a large, powerful adult, so it is essential to supervise interactions with small children – no matter how trustworthy your Rottweiler appears to be.

At the other end of the age spectrum, the Rottweiler may not be the breed of choice for those getting on in years, or with physical disabilities. Obviously, good training is the key to having a well behaved dog no matter his size – but the sheer power of the Rottweiler may be too much of a challenge.

The versatile Rottweiler

This is a highly intelligent breed that needs to use his brain.

During the First and Second World Wars, Rottweilers were put into service in various roles, working as messenger, draught, and guard dogs. Today, they are often used as search and rescue dogs, assistance dogs, guide dogs for the blind, therapy dogs, guard and police dogs.

However, the vast majority of Rottweilers are companion dogs, and although they suit this role admirably, most require extra mental stimulation.

This can be provided in many different ways, from teaching basic obedience and inventing new tricks and exercises for your Rottweiler to perform, to getting involved in more advanced training. If you are interested in competing in one of the canine sports, such as obedience, agility, working trials or tracking, look no further! The Rottweiler excels in all these disciplines, and working closely with your Rottweiler will enrich your relationship and build a closer bond.

Below: With the right training and socialization, the Rottweiler will be a loyal and loving member of the family.

Tracing back in time

The origin of Rottweilers is not well documented, but it is believed that they are descended from the Roman cattle dogs or drovers, making them one of the oldest herding breeds in history.

The Roman legions would have travelled with their meat 'on the hoof' and therefore needed dogs to herd the cattle, as well as guard the livestock at night against dangers such as wolves or cattle rustlers. One route the army travelled was through Württemberg and on to the small market town of Rottweil. This town was populated by the Romans between AD81 and AD96 and was named Area Flaviae after the Flavian Emperor Vespasian.

The town was rebuilt by the Romans with stone buildings and was named Rote Wil (meaning Red Villa) after the red-colored tiles used on the roofs of the more important buildings of the Roman

settlement. From this, the name of the town eventually changed to Rottweil.

This region eventually became an important cattle area, and the descendants of the Roman cattle dogs mixed with local dogs the Romans met on their travels. These included Mollosser dogs from England and the Netherlands, which proved their worth in both driving and protecting the cattle from robbers and wild animals. The butchers and cattle dealers found this herding dog ideal, and from this stemmed a trade in purposely-bred working dogs, based in Rottweil. To celebrate the good qualities of the breed, the dogs that came from Rottweil were called Rottweilers.

The Swiss connection

Roman droving dogs also settled in Switzerland and their characteristics were altered to suit the particular area they populated. These dogs are known as Sennenhunds, four of which include the Appenzellar, the Entlebucher, the Bernese Mountain Dog and the Greater Swiss Mountain Dog. It is believed that the Rottweiler is distantly related to the Sennenhunds and, indeed, when you study the Breed Standards for these dogs, you can see similarities to the Rottweiler of today.

The Bernese Mountain Dog, one of the Sennenhunds, may have played a part in the Rottweiler's development.

The all-rounder

The Rottweiler was first and foremost used for herding cattle and pigs, although dogs of this type were also used for herding sheep. It was a hard task to drive the animals and to keep them together at the same time. The work required a strong dog with high stamina, both mentally and physically, but which also had the energy and courage to impose his own will on obstinate cattle.

Reliable, calm, full of self-will and physical strength, the Rottweiler knew how to cope. He would move the cattle by using his body strength and weight to lean against them – a trait that can often be seen in their ancestors as they lean into you for a fuss. The more rebellious animals would be nipped at the heels until they obeyed.

The qualities of these dogs quickly became known and they became sought after by foreign visitors. Known as the Rottweiler Metzgerhund (Rottweil's butcher's dog), he was not only employed for driving cattle, but was also very useful for pulling the carts of farmers, butchers, bakers and pedlars.

In addition, the Rottweiler was an incredible guard dog; it is thought that the cattle dealers secured the payment for their herds to their collars on the return journey, as there would have been few people brave enough to challenge these courageous dogs.

However, by the end of the 19th century, the railway became the main method for moving stock to market, and a new law was brought in, banning the driving of cattle by dog. Donkeys were now being used to pull the carts and, as a result, the Rottweiler was largely neglected by the people of Rottweil. It is reported that the numbers dwindled until, by 1900, there was only one bitch to be found in Rottweil itself.

Facing page:
The Rottweiler needed to be strong and powerful with high levels of endurance.

Developing the breed

At the beginning of the 20th century, the Rottweiler was close to extinction. But the drive and character found in the breed came to its rescue.

In 1910 the Rottweiler was officially recognized as the fourth dog breed of the German Police Dog Association, which gave it a new lease of life. The first two Rottweiler recruits were Max von der Strahlenberg and Flock von Hamburg. This new role allowed the breed to flourish once again.

The first Rottweiler club in Germany, named DRK (Deutscher Rottweiler-Klub or German Rottweiler Club) was formed on January 13th 1907, followed by the creation of the SDRK (Süddeutscher Rottweiler-Klub or South German Rottweiler Club) on 27 April 1907, which became the IRK (International Rottweiler Club). The DRK registered around 500 Rottweilers, the SDRK some 3,000 Rottweilers.

The goals of the two clubs were different. The DRK wanted to produce working dogs and the IRK tried to produce a uniform look according to the Breed Standard laid down.

The various German Rottweiler clubs amalgamated in 1921 to form the Allgemeiner Deutscher Rottweiler Klub (ADRK), which is recognized worldwide as the home club of the Rottweiler.

The Rottweiler goes global

The outstanding qualities of the Rottweiler have been universally recognized, and throughout the world the breed is valued as a show dog, a working dog and as a companion.

The American Kennel Club first registered a Rottweiler in 1931 when a bitch was imported from Germany by August Knecht, followed by a dog, Arras V, Gerbermuhle. In Britain, the first Rottweiler arrived in 1936 when Thelma Gray, an international judge of all breeds, imported a bitch called Diana v.d. Amalieuburg. She imported a second bitch, Enne von Pfalzgau, which was in whelp, and one of the resulting puppies, Anna from Rozavael, went on to be highly successful in working trials and in the show ring.

The outbreak of World War Two put a stop to further development, and progress was slow for many years

It was the Rottweiler's outstanding working abilities that ensured his survival.

with only a few imports which did little to establish the breed. However, that changed dramatically from the 1960s onwards when the breed quite literally soared in popularity. This is seen most dramatically in US statistics; only 58 Rottweilers were registered with the AKC in 1958 but that figure had grown to over 100,000 by the 1990s.

This trend was also seen in the UK, although on a smaller scale, and also in Australia, where the first two imports did not arrive until 1962.

The breed went from strength to strength in its newly adopted countries, and some fine show dogs and working dogs were produced, along with companion dogs of good character. However, as is so often the case, too many Rottweilers were produced to meet the growing demand, and temperament began to suffer. This powerful breed, which is valued for its fearless reputation, began to attract adverse publicity, mostly because dogs fell into the wrong hands and were not given the training and socialization that is so essential for this breed.

Sadly, the Rottweiler fell into disrepute and it is only through the tireless work of true breed enthusiasts that it is once again finding its place in society.

What should a Rottweiler look like?

For each recognised breed of dog, there is a Breed Standard, which is drawn up by breed specialists to create a picture in words of the 'perfect' dog. It describes the mental and physical characteristics that a breed needs to perform the function for which it was developed, and it describes the breed's looks, movement and temperament.

Breeders strive to produce a dog that most closely conforms to the Breed Standard, and at dog shows, judges examine the dogs and place them according to how closely each dog compares with their own interpretation of the 'perfect' dog as described in the breed's official Standard.

Dog Expert 1 57

This is of immense importance as it is the dogs that win in the show ring that will be responsible for producing future generations of the breed.

General appearance

A medium to large breed, the Rottweiler is a powerful dog. His size and build demonstrates great strength and physical endurance. These traits would have been required to work cattle, which would probably have been wilder than modern-day livestock.

Characteristics and temperament

The Rottweiler is a calm and self-confident dog. He will have an inherent desire to guard both his home and family. It is most important that this instinct is never encouraged, as it can quickly get out of control. He is good-natured and should not be nervous, shy or too excitable. Often, a Rottweiler will want to follow family members around the house, as the breed loves to be around people. They are very intelligent and enjoy training.

The description of temperament is, for me, one of the most important parts of the Breed Standard. A dog with so much size, strength and power must have a good-natured temperament in order to live happily alongside his family.

Points of anatomy

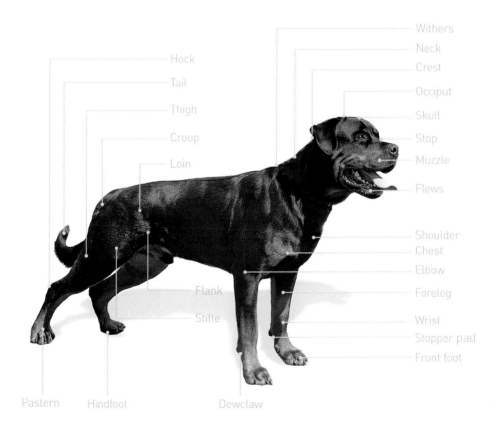

Hock

Tail

Thigh

Croup

Loin

Flank

Stifle

Pastern

Hindfoot

Dewclaw

Withers

Neck

Crest

Occiput

Skull

Stop

Muzzle

Flews

Shoulder

Chest

Elbow

Foreleg

Wrist

Stopper pad

Front foot

Head and skull

The head is probably the main feature that distinguishes the Rottweiler from other breeds. The top of the skull should be broad between the ears and well muscled, giving the impression of power and substance.

Correct male heads have a 'character' to them, and should give the impression of overall masculinity. The female head may have slightly softer angles.

The top skull should have a slight arch from the stop (the angle from the nose to the skull) to the occipital ridge (the point at the base of the skull) and from ear to ear, but not too arched as to give a domed effect. The skull should only make up 60 per cent of the length from tip of nose to occipital ridge. The stop should be well pronounced in the male head.

The muzzle should be of a length that makes up the further 40 percent of the overall length of the head. The skin should be smooth and not loose, although quite often you will see a few wrinkles appear on the top of a Rottweiler's head when he is attentive or alert.

Eyes

The eyes should be dark brown in color; anything
lighter is considered undesirable. This is not so
much a health reason, as the eyes can work just
as well regardless of the color, but it is
an all-important trait. As the eye
color gets lighter, it softens
the appearance of the gaze,
losing the fearlessness of
the Rottweiler expression.

*Right: The head is
strong and noble
with dark eyes which
give an impression of
fearlessness.*

The shape of the eyes should be almond and not round, and should lie at a 10 to 15-degree angle above the bridge of the nose, preferably set wide apart. The eyelids should be tight fitting.

Ears

The ears should be the shape of an equilateral triangle and should sit close to the cheek, with the bottom tip lying flat to the cheek and not curling out. The ear set should increase the overall appearance of the size of the Rottweiler's head while remaining in proportion with it.

Mouth

The Rottweiler has strong, large teeth, which should meet in a scissor bite (which is where the upper teeth slightly overlap the lower teeth evenly. The lips should always be black and firm – not flopping down like a Bloodhound's. Ideally, the gums should also have black coloring, although many Rottweilers do have pink gums.

Neck

In order to support and carry a Rottweiler's magnificent head, the neck needs to be of a fair length and very muscular. The correct appearance would be slightly arched and free from dewlaps.

Body

The front legs should be straight, muscular, with plenty of bone and substance, and the pasterns (the part between the foot and the leg) should slope slightly forward. The elbows should sit well under the body and not stick out or turn in. This will also determine the feet, which should be straight, not standing at an angle, often referred to as the 'ten to two' position.

Below: The ears should lie close to the cheek.

The chest is broad and deep, with a straight back that is strong and not too long. The shoulder should be in proportion to the length of body. The loins should be short, strong and deep. The croup (area near the tail) should be in proportion to the body and very slightly sloping.

As it is the back end that powers this breed, the muscles in the hindquarters should be well developed both in the upper and lower thigh. The stifles or knees should be fairly well angulated and not straight.

Feet

The feet should be round and compact with toes well arched, giving an overall neat look. The hind feet are somewhat longer than the front feet. The toenails should be short and dark in color.

Tail

The Rottweiler is among a number of breeds of dogs whose tails were traditionally docked from birth.

No one really knows why the Rottweiler's tail was originally docked, but there are a number of theories.

Despite his size, the Rottweiler should be active and agile.

Some say it may have been linked to taxes imposed on dogs. Working dogs may have been exempt from these taxes, and docking the dog's tail could have been a way of proving he was indeed a working dog. Others say they were docked to avoid possible damage that may be inflicted by working so closely alongside boisterous cattle.

Nowadays, the only reason for docking Rottweilers is for cosmetic purposes, and it is banned in many countries. However, docking is still allowed in the USA.

The Rottweiler was customarily docked – but this was purely for cosmetic purposes.

Below: Tail carriage is not yet standardised in the breed, but there is no doubt that the Rottweiler uses his full tail as an important means of communication.

Gait/ Movement

As the Rottweiler was initially bred to herd cattle, the overall movement should show off his strength and endurance. The best way to see a Rottweiler move is in the trot. He should be able to move freely, without showing any signs of lameness, and, when you watch him move, most of the power will come from the rear end while the front legs stride out purposefully. His back should remain straight and balanced at all times.

Coat

The Rottweiler is a double-coated breed, which means that he has both a medium length top coat and an undercoat. The top coat is coarse to the touch.

Color

A Rottweiler is predominantly black with clearly defined rich, tan markings, which should not cover more than 10 per cent of the whole body. The markings are set out specifically as with all black-and-tan dogs as follows:

- A spot over each eye and on each cheek.

- A strip around each side of muzzle and on the throat.

- Two clear triangles on either side of the breast bone, giving the appearance of a bow when looking from the front.

- Marking down the front legs towards the toes, which often have smudged black markings.

- On the inside of the hind legs, but not completely eliminating black from the back of the legs and under the tail.

Some Rottweilers are born with white markings, which is classed as a breed fault. However, a lot of puppies born with white hairs often shed them as they grow. The undercoat can be grey, fawn or black.

Size

Rottweilers vary in size between dogs and bitches. There is a guideline set out of the ideal size for both as follows: dogs' height at shoulder between 25 and 27 in (63-69 cm) and bitches between 23 and 25 in (58-64 cm). This is only a guideline, as I have seen both dogs and bitches outside these measurements and, unless you want to show your dog, the size does not affect the overall health of your pet in any way.

Facing page: Tan markings should be restricted to 10 percent of the body color.

What do you want from your Rottweiler?

The Rottweiler is one of the most versatile of all dog breeds and will excel in most fields. However, it is important that you decide what you want from your dog so that he lives up to your expectations, and you give him the lifestyle and training he needs.

Companion dog

Most Rottweiler puppies go to pet homes, and so the overriding considerations are health and temperament.

Obviously you want a healthy dog but also, equally important, a dog that is sound in temperament.

This comes from his genetic make-up, so you need to check out his family background as thoroughly as possible – and the rest is down to you. The Rottweiler has a superb temperament, but this is a breed that must have firm, fair and consistent handling.

Working dog

Some owners know right from the start that they want to compete with their dog in one of the canine sports, such as obedience, tracking, working trials, or agility. The Rottweiler is a highly intelligent dog and, with the right training, most will achieve a good standard in whatever discipline you choose.

With the correct training and socialization, the Rottweiler has an impeccable temperament.

Show dog

If you want to buy a puppy with the aim of showing him, you will need to research the Breed Standard to get a good idea of what qualities to look out for. If you express this desire to the breeder, they will help you to choose the puppy with the most potential.

Bear in mind that there is no guarantee that a puppy with show potential will grow into a successful show dog. Youngsters can change considerably as they mature, so all you can go on is how the puppy looks at the time you are choosing him. It is also helpful if you see close relatives so you can form a picture of the type of Rottweiler a particular breeder produces.

Guard dog

The Rottweiler has natural guarding instincts when he matures, but this has proved to be a double-edged sword. Too many people have been attracted to the breed for the wrong reasons, wanting to enhance their own image with a 'macho' dog, or taking on a Rottweiler in the belief that he will guard home and family, without any training.

In fact, the Rottweiler's willingness to guard property is not guaranteed. This is not a breed that will flourish being chained up in a garden or used solely as a guard dog. Should you want to protect your property, you would be better off investing in a more reliable alternative, such as a burglar alarm or CCTV. A Rottweiler enjoys being with his family too much to thrive on this kind of life.

What your Rottweiler wants from you

Dog ownership is a life-long commitment so the decision to bring a Rottweiler into your home should not be made lightly.

Before buying a Rottweiler, you should research the breed so you know what they are taking on. Every person within the household should be committed to their share in his upbringing and care.

Time

Your Rottweiler will be miserable – and possibly
destructive – if he is left for long periods on his own.
A dog should never be left for more than four hours
at a stretch. If work commitments pose a problem,
you will need to make alternative arrangements,
such as hiring a dog sitter or a dog walker.

Training and socialization

The Rottweiler also needs to undergo an extensive
programme of socialization, so that he is able to
cope calmly and confidently in all situations.

Exercise requirements

A Rottweiler needs an hour of exercise every day
and some kind of mental stimulation or training to
exercise his brain as well as his body.

Make sure you give
your Rottweiler the
time and attention
he deserves.

Extra
considerations

Now you have decided that the Rottweiler is the breed for you, you need to narrow your choice, so know exactly what your are looking for. This will help in your search to find the ideal dog to suit your lifestyle

Male or female?

The choice of male of female is a matter of personal preference, but there are some important considerations to bear in mind.

A male Rottweiler can grow up to 27 inches (69 cm) and weigh up to 126 lb (57 kg). Although very loving with his family, a male can be assertive with other dogs and pass through different stages of maturity with noticeable behavior changes.

If you have no plans to breed from your male Rottweiler, you would do well to consider neutering.

Neutering has a number of health benefits, as well making the dog easier to live with. Ask your vet for further advice.

A female Rottweiler is usually smaller and lighter. Unlike the males, you will usually find that what you have from a young puppy is generally what you end up with in an adult. Generally, she will be more biddable than a male and breeders will suggest that someone who has little or no experience of the breed should have a female, as they are much easier to handle.

If you take on a female, you will need to cope with her seasonal cycle unless you have her neutered. Opinions vary as to when is the best time to do this, so ask your vet for advice.

Below: The male (right) is bigger and stronger than the female (left).

More than one?

More than one puppy in the house causes double the workload, requires double the time spent training each dog, and costs double the money in food, toys and vet bills. You may also find that the two puppies may bond so closely with each other that they may not care about the rest of the family unit.   Alternatively, as they grow up, they may compete with each other and this can cause problems with aggression.

If you want to add to your numbers, wait until your first dog is at least 18 months old, and fully trained, before taking on a new puppy.

Resist the temptation
of getting two puppies
from the same litter.

Puppy or older rescued dog?

It is a sad fact of life that many Rottweilers, through no fault of their own, end up in welfare organizations looking for a new forever home. You may want to weigh up the pros and cons between a puppy and a rescued dog.

If you take on a puppy, he comes with a relatively clean slate but he brings a degree of upheaval to your home. You will have accidents around the house, personal belongings may be chewed and destroyed and, in the early days, you may have some sleepless nights.

The older rescued dog will usually have basic training; many may just require some additional training to polish the edges. Older dogs will usually be house-trained and are less likely to destroy things. The only downside is that you may not know their history. Some rescued dogs may require specialist training or may have a health problem that needs managing.

If, as a family, you decide that the older dog is for you, there are a number of welfare organizations, some of which are dedicated specifically to the Rottweiler, who can help you find a dog that will suit your family and your situation.

Facing page: If you take on a rescued dog, try to find out about his history.

Sourcing a puppy

Where are you going to find a Rottweiler puppy that is sound, healthy and typical of the breed?

Places to avoid

Avoid a breeder who sells lots of different breeds of puppies. This could well indicate that the aim is to make as much money as possible rather than giving a lifetime's dedication to one special breed.

Puppy farms are run by unscrupulous breeders, who house adult dogs, often in appalling conditions, with no exercise or human interaction. Puppies are churned out with little or no consideration for the health of the mother dog or the puppies themselves. The puppies may be very young when they are taken from the mother, so will miss out on essential socialization, which will have a detrimental effect on their future development.

*You may have to wait
some time to get the
ideal puppy.*

Finding a reputable breeder

The best way to find a decent breeder is by contacting your national Kennel Club for details of Rottweiler breed clubs in your area. Secretaries of breed clubs will have contact details of local breeders and may know who has puppies available.

Once you have a list of breeders, make several phone calls and do not be afraid to ask questions. A responsible breeder should find the time to answer all your queries as well as giving you information about the puppies they have bred. You should ask the breeder about the temperament of their lines and the socialization the puppies have received.

In the hot seat

A reputable breeder will want to vet you, so be prepared to be questioned before you get the go-ahead to buy a puppy. The breeder will want to know about your home and family set-up, and if you plan to get involved in showing or any of the dog sports. Do not be intimidated by such breeders: they want what is best for the breed and for their dogs.

Health issues

Like all breeds, the Rottweiler does have some inherited health issues, so the first question you should ask the breeder is if the dam (mother) and sire (father) have had the relevant health checks. For the Rottweiler, this should include tests for hip dysplasia and elbow dysplasia; eye testing is a bonus.

For information on inherited and breed disposed disorders, see page 156

For information on inherited and breed disposed disorders, see page 156

Below: You need to find a breeder that has a reputation for producing typical Rottweilers with sound temperaments.

Puppy watching

Rottweiler puppies are like little woolly teddy bears and they are totally irresistible. However, you are only going to take one puppy home with you, so how do you make sure you pick the perfect pup?

The best time to visit is when the puppies are about five weeks old, as they are then mobile and their characters will be forming. You should expect to visit the puppies at least twice before taking your puppy home.

Ideally, the puppies should be in the breeder's home from the beginning, rather than in a kennel, as it is important that they experience the day-to-day activities that go on in the house.

The puppies should appear happy and healthy with bright eyes showing no discharge, and healthy,

shiny coats without signs of baldness or sores on the skin. It is important to see the mother with her puppies as this will give you some idea of the temperament they are likely to inherit.

The mother should be friendly and you should ask to interact with her even if only to make a fuss of her. If the breeder is reluctant to let you do this, there may be an issue with temperament, so walk away! Although the male's genes contribute to the overall temperament of the puppies, the mother's close contact and influence plays a great part in the development of the puppies' characters.

Sometimes the breeder will own the father, although this is rare, as quite often the male is from another kennel and from different bloodlines. However, you should be able to see photos of the stud dog, and check out his pedigree, his show record, and make sure he has been health tested.

The right choice

The puppies should approach you, sniff you and then act confidently around you. Remember that puppies do chew and bite, so seeing this behavior does not mean that they are going to be aggressive.

Spend some time with the puppies and only make your decision if you are truly happy with the way the

puppies act and look. Remember that all puppies are cute and it is often our instinct to rescue ill-looking or unhappy-looking puppies. This is done at a potentially high cost to you at a later date. If you have any concerns about health, ask your vet to come and visit the puppies. If you cannot arrange this, ask the breeder if they are prepared to offer you a full refund within 48 hours of taking the puppy, and get the puppy checked by your vet when you first take him home.

Show puppy

If you have plans to show your Rottweiler, the breeder will help you to pick out a puppy that has the correct conformation, movement and markings at this early stage.

Ideally, you want a puppy that has strong bone and substance along with a good head with a short, broad muzzle. The eyes should be dark, as should the pigment around the mouth. The puppy should have good, straight front legs when standing alert. The colors should be black and a rich mahogany without any trace of white in the coat, as this is classed as a breed fault. The coat itself should be short and not wavy. The chances are, if the parents are from good show stock, the puppies are likely to inherit the correct conformation.

Facing page: Sometimes there is a puppy who seems to say: "pick me!".

A Rottweiler-friendly home

It will soon be time to bring your Rottweiler puppy home, but before you do this, there is much to plan in advance and consider.

House rules

First of all, decide all the ground rules before the puppy comes into your home, and make sure that the whole family sticks to the same rules. A puppy needs consistent handling by everyone or he will very quickly become confused.

Rottweilers are very much people dogs. They like to follow their owners around the house and will often just lie in the room that you happen to be in. If, for whatever reason, you do not want your dog to do this, he must be dissuaded from doing so from the beginning. This can be easily achieved by using stair gates to block off restricted areas.

Safety in the home

Check your home to ensure that your little pup will be safe. All puppies chew, so any wires that are on show should be secured, or the area needs to be one that your puppy is not allowed to access. Cleaning materials and detergents should be shut away in cupboards as they are potentially lethal if ingested by an inquisitive puppy. Make sure that children's toys are not left around, as these can potentially be harmful to a puppy, which likes to test everything with his mouth. The same goes for smaller articles of clothing.

In the garden

The garden must be surrounded by secure fencing which should be at least 6 ft (1.8 m) in height. It is essential that you walk the perimeter of the fence to check for any holes that your puppy can get through. Being naturally curious animals, they will take these escape routes to explore.

If you have plants in your garden and you are fond of them, you will need to fence off an area to prevent your puppy from getting to them. Rottweilers are great diggers and will have endless fun ripping up your prize perennials and burying toys and bones in their place. Also watch out for plants that are poisonous to dogs; lists can be found on the Internet.

Finding a vet

It is a good idea to register with a vet before you collect your puppy. Consult friends who own dogs. Breed clubs can also provide lists of recommended vets, including, in some cases, veterinarians with special knowledge of particular breeds.

Buying equipment

It is essential to buy everything you need prior to your puppy or older dog coming home. If you choose wisely, the equipment will last for many years.

Sleeping quarters

Rottweiler puppies can be very destructive and a fabric bed could become shredded over the course of time. A plastic bed that is lined with some vet bedding (synthetic fleece-style bedding) is ideal.

I highly recommend dog owners buying a crate and training your puppy to sleep in it from the first day. The crate should be large enough to house an adult Rottweiler stretched out, but initially it should be set up so that the bed is placed in one half and the other half lined with newspaper to provide a toilet area. Arrange a sheet or blanket across the top of the crate to make it more den-like.

Crate training can begin from day one. Start by feeding your dog or puppy all of his meals in his crate, and encourage him to sleep in there with the door open. It is essential that he never considers being put in his crate as a punishment. This has to be an area where he feels safe and secure.

Bowls

Your new puppy will need a bowl for both his food and his water. The safest type is one made of stainless steel, which is easy to clean and your puppy will be unable to chew and destroy it.

Collar and lead

Your puppy will grow at an alarming rate and the initial puppy collar and lead set will probably only last a few weeks. The collar should fit snugly against your dog's neck; you should be able to fit two fingers between the collar and his neck.

As your puppy grows, you will need to buy a bigger, slightly wider collar; one that is about an inch (2.5 cm) wide is perfectly sufficient. There are two types of collar I would recommend: a flat collar with a buckle (not a snap fastener, as these can come apart at a crucial moment), or a half-check collar. A half-check collar is made of either leather or nylon, which is connected by a chain that tightens if your dog pulls.

The lead should allow your dog to walk comfortably at your side; about 3 ft (1 metre) in length is ideal and it should be made of a good-quality leather or nylon.

Identification

When your Rottweiler is out in public places, he needs to have some form of ID. Pet stores, supermarkets and some veterinary practices sell dog tags and will engrave them with your contact details. You may also wish to consider a permanent form of ID – either microchipping or tattooing your dog.

Toys

Rottweilers like nothing more than to play and interact with their owners. When choosing toys for your puppy or older dog, you will need to find things that are tough and durable.

Balls are great fun, but make sure it is one with a rope attached, and always check regularly for damage. Rottweilers also like soft toys, but be careful if choosing these types of toys, as they can be ripped apart in no time, and if the stuffing is ingested it can cause serious problems.

Tug toys are also very good for the Rottweiler, as this encourages play and interaction with you, thus strengthening the bond between you. However, this type of game is best avoided with a young puppy, especially during the teething stages, as it could cause pain.

If you are going out and want to leave your Rottweiler with something to amuse himself, then a Kong (a hollow, rubber, cone-shaped toy, which can be filled with something tasty) is probably one of the best objects to keep him occupied. These can be bought in most pet shops or via the Internet.

Grooming Gear

Initially, all you need is a soft brush so your puppy gets used to being groomed. This can be replaced with a rubber brush when the adult coat comes through.

Settling in

The big day has finally come and it is time to go and collect your puppy. Check with the breeder if you can arrive in the morning, to allow your puppy time to settle once he is home. If possible, ask for a piece of bedding that has a smell familiar to the puppy that you can take home with you, as this will help to make the transition as stress free as possible.

Once your puppy arrives in his new home, try to keep the environment as quiet as possible. Avoid having too many people crowding him – your friends can always come and meet your new Rottweiler another day, once he is settled in. Let your puppy explore the areas of the house and garden that will be his environment. Although tempting, try not to lavish too much attention on your puppy too quickly; this is a scary situation for him and he needs time to get used to both the environment and his new family.

Facing page:
At last the waiting is
over and it is time to
take your puppy home.

Meeting the family

Rottweilers and children can live together harmoniously as long as both parties understand the rules. It is important to remember that a puppy is not a toy for your children and should not be carried around like a doll or a teddy bear. Puppies' bones are very soft and a child can easily damage joints by accidentally dropping, or falling on, a pup.

All puppies test with their teeth and although undesirable, nipping is perfectly natural behavior. Littermates bite each other and play rough, and your puppy will probably think that his new human family will carry on with these games. Children should learn that when the puppy does nip, they should say "Ouch" and then walk away, telling the puppy in a language that he understands that this is not the way to behave.

Involve all family members with the day-to-day care of your puppy and this will enable the bond to develop with the whole family as opposed to just one person. Encourage the children to train and reward the puppy, teaching him to follow their commands without question.

The animal family

I have always introduced my existing dogs to a new puppy before the puppy actually comes home. Dogs learn a lot through smell, so make sure that when you visit your puppy at the breeder, he gets a chance to smell the other animals on you. Cuddle him to you throughout the visit and, when you go home, allow your existing dogs to have a good sniff of you and your clothing while you make a gentle fuss of them. If you can do this on more than one occasion, all the better.

On the day you bring the puppy home, sit with your puppy on your lap and let your other dog have a sniff and satisfy his curiosity, again calmly stroking him. The most important thing is not to discipline the older dog, but to encourage him to be gentle around the puppy.

Care should be taken at mealtimes, and you should prevent your puppy from trying to take food from your older dog. The safest measure here would be to feed both dogs separately until they are used to each other. I would always recommend that all interactions between your dog and your new puppy should be supervised until such a time as they have established their relationship.

Facing page:
Allow a puppy and an
older dog to work out
their own relationship.

If you are taking on an older, rescued dog then introductions with existing dogs should be on neutral ground on a lead, long before the newest member of the family is brought home. Most reputable welfare organizations will insist on this to ensure your rescue Rottweiler has a smooth transition into his new home.

Meeting a cat should be supervised in a similar way, but do not allow your puppy to be rough with it. Most cats are more than capable of looking after themselves, but care must be taken at the first meeting to prevent any unwanted animosity, as this will only progress as the puppy grows. Given time and supervision, there is no reason why a Rottweiler cannot live very happily with a cat.

Rottweilers possess quite a high prey drive and small animals such as hamsters and rabbits could quite easily become the object of prey for your puppy. Again, allowing the puppy to sniff the small animal, making himself familiar with it, will help, but care must be taken at all times to ensure that the small animal is never left out of a secure cage or pen when your Rottweiler is around. Instinct is a very hard thing for him to battle against, so you need to ensure that your puppy does not get into the habit of chasing smaller animals.

Feeding

Most breeders will provide a diet sheet for you to follow and usually you will be given a small bag of food to take home with you. It is important that you follow this diet sheet for the first few weeks, as this will help the settling-in period to go smoothly.

If you want to change the brand of dog food your pup is being fed, you will need to do this gradually by mixing some of the new food with his existing diet and then slowly increasing the amount of the new food and decreasing the old. Watch carefully for any changes in your dog's behavior and toilet, as the new food may not be suitable and you might have to consider rethinking his diet.

The first night

Your puppy will have spent the first weeks of his life either with his mother or curled up with his siblings. He is then taken from everything he knows as familiar and is often lavished with attention by his new family for several hours. Then comes bed time. It is at this time that he is placed in his crate, all the lights are switched off, and he is abandoned – at least that is how he feels. This is why puppies howl at night – not always through distress, as we often interpret, but howling is an effective means for a dog to call his pack to locate it. Dogs are pack animals and like to be with their family.

I prefer to have the crate in my bedroom at night so that the puppy is always with his family. After the first few nights you can then start to move the crate out of the bedroom and locate it in a permanent position for nighttime use. I have followed this routine with most of my dogs, and I have never had a problem with sleepless nights. I have also been aware of when the puppy has shown signs of needing to toilet, and have thus been able to take him outside, making house-training that much quicker.

If you decide against this, make sure you do not make a big fuss of your puppy when you leave him. Leave a couple of teddy bears in his bed to represent other

Facing page:
It is inevitable that your puppy will miss the company of his littermates to begin with.

puppies, and leave a radio playing quietly in his room. Make sure that the radio is tuned into talking rather than music, as this will be more soothing to a puppy.

If he howls in the night, the best thing is to ignore him. This could go on for some time and carry on for several nights, so if you are taking this route, it may be an idea to forewarn your neighbors. Going back to a puppy that howls is just rewarding him for this behavior and will encourage him to continue to howl each time he sees fit.

Rescued dogs

Settling an older, rescued dog in the home is very similar to a puppy in as much as you will need to have made the same preparations regarding his homecoming. As with a puppy, an older dog will need you to be consistent, so start as you mean to go on.

There is often a honeymoon period when first bringing a rescued dog home, where he will be on his best behavior for the first few weeks. It is after these first couple of weeks that the true nature of the dog will show, so be prepared for subtle changes in his behavior. Register with a reputable training school so that any problems encountered can be quickly and easily dealt with. Above all, remember that a rescued dog ceases to be a rescued dog the moment he enters his forever home and should be treated normally like any other family member.

Facing page:
A rescued dog
needs kindness and
consideration to
help him settle in
his new home.

Dog Expert 87

House-training

The key to house-training your puppy is to be vigilant and consistent so that you establish a routine your puppy understands. The fewer mistakes he makes, the sooner he will learn to be clean in the house.

The breeder may have started the process of house-training by teaching the puppies to relieve themselves on newspaper, or even in a litter tray. This will have implanted the idea of keeping the nest or bed area clean, and going elsewhere for toileting.

When your puppy arrives in his new home, you can continue this process by moving the paper nearer and nearer to the back door and eventually out to the garden. However, you may prefer to cut out this interim phase and establish a routine of taking your puppy out to the garden at regular intervals.

Dog Experts 89

A small puppy will need to relieve himself at frequent intervals. The best plan is to take him out at the following times:

- First thing in the morning

- After mealtimes

- After waking up from a nap

- After a play session

- Last thing at night.

Do not leave more than two-hour gaps between trips to the garden; hourly outings are ideal if you can manage them.

It helps if you have a designated toileting area in the garden as your puppy will associate it with relieving himself, and it will also help you to clean up after him. When your puppy performs, give him lots of praise and, maybe, a treat, so he knows how pleased you are with him. When he understands what is required, you can use a verbal cue, such as "Be clean" which will be useful for getting a quicker response, and you can also use it when you are away from home.

Do not rush back into the house as soon as your puppy has relieved himself as he might start to employ delaying tactics. Spend a few minutes playing with pup before heading indoors.

When accidents happen

If you catch your puppy soiling in the house, try clapping your hands to startle him and, hopefully, interrupt his toilet. Carry him to the garden and stay with him. Eventually he will need to finish what he started in the house and when he does, praise as above and reward.

You should never scold your puppy for accidents in the house, as all this will do is cause anxieties about toileting. He may worry about relieving himself in front of you, and will find 'secret' places to go in the house. If your puppy has an accident, remember to use a deodorizer to discourage him for using that spot again.

Below: If you establish a routine, your puppy will soon learn to be clean in the house.

Choosing a diet

There is a wide variety of dog food available and the choice can be bewildering. The aim is to find a diet that will suit your dog, and is convenient for you to buy and feed.

Commercial diets

Commercial diets come in the form of canned meat, which is usually served with biscuit, and complete food, which comes in the form of kibble. Generally, dogs find canned food very appetizing, but you need to read the label carefully to check the ingredients. Canned food often has a very high moisture content, and you need to make sure your Rottweiler is getting the nutrition he requires.

A complete diet is scientifically manufactured to cater for all your dog's nutritional needs and should not be supplemented. Many manufacturers produce

diets for different life stages, such as puppy, adult, veteran, or for nursing bitches, and there are some that are designed for particular breeds.

When choosing a complete diet, it is important to study the additives and protein content. I am often faced with hyperactive puppies at my training school, who are flying high, possibly because of foods that are either too high in protein or have too many additives. Check the ingredients, as they are listed in order of highest quantity.

Ideally, your Rottweiler should be on a diet that is mainly meat and backed with a good source of cereal, such as rice or oats. Look for foods that claim to be free from wheat and dairy products, as these are foods often associated with allergies in dogs.

Be aware of price, as a cheap dog food could be lower in quality and it is essential that your Rottweiler puppy has a good-quality diet to encourage healthy growth.

Natural diets

You may decide that you want to feed your dog a raw diet, consisting of raw meat and bones, which you can either purchase from your local butcher or from a meat supplier by post.

If you decide to feed your dog this way, you must remember that dogs are not purely meat eaters and you will need to add fruit and vegetables to the diet. There are several books on the market that explain the raw diet and how to feed it, and I would strongly recommend you learn all about it before adopting this method of feeding

Feeding regime

Rottweiler puppies will initially require feeding four times a day, cutting down to three times when they are about four months old and then down to twice daily from around six months. As the dog grows, so does the stomach, thus enabling you to increase each meal to meet this daily feeding requirement.

I would never feed a Rottweiler any less than twice daily, as feeding too much in one sitting can cause an often-fatal condition called gastric torsion, where gases build up in the stomach, causing it to twist. For the same reason, avoid exercise and play with your Rottweiler for approximately two hours before and after each meal to allow food to settle.

A Rottweiler should not be fat at any time of his development, as carrying too much weight could prove harmful to growing bones.

You should be able to feel the dog's ribs when you run your hands along his sides, but they should not be prominent when your dog is standing relaxed.

Mealtimes

Your puppy's feeding times will be initially guided by the breeder and it is important that you stick to these times as much as possible to ease the settling-in process. Once you start easing off the number of feeds, then the times can be adjusted more to suit your lifestyle. Dogs are creatures of habit and will soon become used to eating at set times. I always vary the times of meals so my dogs are not expecting dinner at a certain time, mainly because I am unable to feed my dogs every day at exactly the same time.

Fresh drinking water should be available to your dog at all times and never withheld for any reason.

Ideal weight

The average weight for the adult Rottweiler is 110 lb (50 kg) for a male and 93 lb (42 kg) for a female, but this is not to say that this weight needs to be achieved by the time the puppy is six months old.

However, a puppy needs the correct amount of food in order that he can develop strong, healthy bones.

Facing page:
The aim is to find a
diet that will suit
your Rottweiler's age
and lifestyle.

An underfed Rottweiler can develop food aggression issues simply because he is hungry. Dog food manufacturers often advise a daily feeding guide; this can be followed as long as you are checking that your puppy is not looking too fat or too thin. If you are unsure at any time, ask your vet for advice. Getting it right at this stage is crucial, as it will determine how your puppy develops.

Bones and chews

Rottweilers love to chew and you can give them something long-lasting, such as a large, rawhide chew, to enjoy for a couple of hours. Never leave your dog with this kind of treat, as I have heard of dogs choking on large pieces that they have tried to swallow whole. Also avoid rawhide chews that have knots at either end, as these can be bitten off and swallowed by your dog and may get stuck in his throat.

A raw meat bone from the butcher is another great treat for your dog, but make sure it is a knuckle bone.

Keep a close check on your Rottweiler's weight as obesity can lead to major health problems.

Caring for your Rottweiler

The Rottweiler is an easy breed to care for in terms of coat care, but you should set time aside on a weekly basis to check him over and attend to his needs.

Grooming

As soon as your puppy has settled in his new home, get him accustomed to grooming. Use a dot brush to work through his coat, and give him lots of praise and a treat when he co-operates.

The adult Rottweiler has a top coat and an undercoat, and will shed his coat twice a year. Use a rubber brush for routine grooming, and when your dog is shedding a coat, you can use a rake which helps remove all the loose undercoat.

© Dog Expert 101

When you are grooming, you can check for any lumps or bumps or for any fleas or ticks that may be making a home on your dog. Should you notice anything out of the ordinary, it is best to get it checked by your vet.

Bathing

Excessive bathing can be harmful for your dog's coat and I would only bath my dogs twice a year at the most. This can be a daunting task, and, if finances permit, I would suggest taking him to a grooming salon, as it will have the facilities to bath and groom your dog, and the experience to do this, with the minimum stress to the animal.

If your dog has rolled in something unpleasant – something all dogs like to do – apply diluted lemon juice on the affected area, which will remove the smell, and, once dry, rinse with warm water. This can be done instead of giving a full bath.

Regular checks

From an early age, your Rottweiler should be accustomed to being examined all over, as you will need to be able to do this throughout his life to check for any irregularities. Start out by using treats; feed your puppy with one hand while, at the same time, running your hand over his body and checking his ears, teeth and feet with the other hand.

Teeth

Rottweiler puppies should have 28 temporary teeth that erupt at about three to four weeks of age. They will eventually have 42 permanent adult teeth that begin to emerge at about three to four months of age. When your Rottweiler is changing from his puppy to his adult teeth, his gums and mouth will be tender and it is best to avoid handling his mouth too much at this time.

Once the adult teeth are in place, it is important to look after them. There are chews on the market designed to loosen plaque and help keep your dog's teeth clean, but it is also important to brush his teeth once or twice a week, using a soft toothbrush and dog toothpaste. Only use toothpaste that is designed for dogs, as human toothpaste can be harmful if swallowed.

Ears

Check your Rottweiler's ears on a monthly basis, and if they are dirty you can use an ear-cleaning solution which you can buy from your vet.

Soak a piece of cotton-wool with this solution and wipe around the inside of the ear. Never go deeper than your first knuckle when doing this.

The shortcoated Rottweiler needs little more than a weekly brush.

You can clean your Rottweiler's ears, but do not probe into the ear canal

Make sure you restrict trimming to the tip of the nail.

Regular teeth cleaning will help prevent the build-up of tartar.

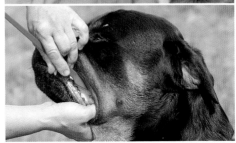

Nails

It is important to cut your Rottweiler's nails. This should be done every two or three weeks. Nails that are allowed to grow too long will force your dog's toes to splay and could result in lameness.

Rottweilers tend to have sensitive feet, so you will need to hold his feet, gently feeling in between his toes, while feeding him treats to make him believe he is having a good experience. This needs to be done right from the beginning.

Because a Rottweiler's nails are black, they are not easy to trim, as you are not able to see where the quick or blood vessel is. If you do cut through the quick, you will cause him pain and, most importantly, he will remember this experience and may not be so keen to allow you to trim his nails in the future.

The safest way to trim nails is to hold your dog's foot securely and clip just under the curve of the nail, removing tiny pieces at a time. Do not forget the dewclaws, which are located further up your Rottweiler's legs.

Exercising your Rottweiler

The Rottweiler is a working dog and is not happy to just laze around the house. He will want daily exercise and training to keep his mind and body

This is an energetic
breed that requires
physical exercise
coupled with mental
stimulation.

stimulated and ensure he remains a stable and pleasurable companion.

Rottweilers need exercise for a variety of reasons. Daily exercise will help to keep your Rottweiler at the correct weight and will also help prevent unwanted behavior, such as chewing and digging, brought on by boredom. Daily walks in a busy environment are an ideal way to socialize your Rottweiler and will also help deepen the bond between you.

While your puppy is growing, exercise must be limited, as he could damage his developing joints. For the same reason, you should prevent your puppy from jumping in and out of the car, and running up and down stairs.

Until your Rottweiler puppy is fully grown, walking should be restricted to no more than two 20-minute walks each day. Make the most of these outings by exposing your pup to many different environments.

Once fully grown, you will need to walk your Rottweiler for about an hour each day. Until you are sure that your dog will come back to you every time you call him, he should not be let off his lead.

Rottweilers love water and will enjoy an outing to the beach, river or lake where he can swim and play in the water. Do be careful of currents and tides, and do not exhaust your dog by endlessly throwing a ball into the water when he is not used to it.

Playing with your Rottweiler

Playing with your Rottweiler not only provides an excellent source of exercise but also strengthens the bond between dog and owner. Rottweilers like nothing more than a game of tug or to have a ball thrown for them to chase. Use a food reward to offer as a swap, so that your dog is always happy to give you his toy, and make sure that as soon as he has done this, the game continues either by throwing the ball again or restarting the tug game. He will learn from this not to become toy aggressive, as it is more fun to share.

Never play wrestling games with your Rottweiler, as it could bring out aggression and he will not know with whom he is allowed to play this game. You would not want your adult Rottweiler jumping on a child, thinking he is playing a game.

The older Rottweiler

As your Rottweiler reaches his twilight years, you will find that he requires less exercise. From about the age of seven, you will find that his muscle tone will be harder to maintain and he will start developing grey hairs around the muzzle.

He will seem content to spend more time sleeping and less time playing.

An older Rottweiler may develop arthritis in later years and you will notice that he may be stiff when getting up off his bed. If you can keep his joints supple by maintaining gentle exercise, this will help. It is also advisable to watch his weight to keep extra pressure off stiff or aching joints. Supplements can be bought to aid arthritis, but you should discuss what is best with your vet, as pain medication is often required.

Incontinence is something that the older dog may face, but your vet can usually prescribe medication for this. Your Rottweiler may develop loss of hearing or his sight may become affected. As with humans, this is something that should be tolerated by the family with patience and respect. If your Rottweiler starts to lose his sight, try to keep furniture in the same place so as not to confuse him.

Letting go

It is a sad fact of life that only a small number of dogs die in their sleep and, as such, it is likely that you will at some point have to make the difficult decision to say goodbye to your beloved Rottweiler. This is the one time where you cannot be selfish and must think of his needs. Your dog will usually tell you when the time has come, by showing an unwillingness to eat, walk or leave his bed. Looking into his eyes, you will see that the sparkle has gone. You must let him go with his dignity.

If you do not want to face the ordeal of going to the surgery, a vet will come to your home. It is the very last thing you will do for your companion, so you must stay with him, reassuring him that all is well until the very end. It is the least you can do to repay him for all the fun and enjoyment he has given you over the years.

Allow your oldie to take as much exercise as he is comfortable with.

Given time, you will be able to look back with fondness on the times you shared, and laugh at some of the antics you both got up to. I would never give up the pleasure of owning a Rottweiler, as the good memories that are created far outweigh the grief of losing your dog.

Although you can never replace a beloved pet, you can replace the relationship and fun times you had with him, so maybe in time you can consider getting another dog to share your life with.

Understanding your Rottweiler

Every dog is an individual and, over a period of time, you will reach a true understanding with your Rottweiler. You will know when he is in high spirits, when he feels worried, or when he is simply clowning around. You will discover all this by observation, but it will help if you have some knowledge of the developmental stages your Rottweiler is going through, as this will help with training and with problem solving.

Dogs can learn throughout their lives, but the period from when they are about seven weeks to sixteen weeks is an optimum time as they will absorb information very quickly. This also means that you must ensure that their experiences during this time

Dog Expert

are positive because, as easily as they learn the behaviors you want, they can also learn negative behaviors. Lots of different changes occur as dogs mature and you will notice that stages described below overlap.

Birth to 6 weeks

The neonatal, transitional, awareness, and primary socialization phases occur during this time. It is important for your puppy to remain with his mother and siblings as it now that he begins to develop canine social skills and establish relationships with his littermates and with his mother. His mother will teach him his first social skills such as play and bite inhibition. It is important that puppies do not leave their mother too early (before seven weeks) because this can have a life-long effect on their behavior with other dogs.

During this phase a puppy begins to form social relationships with other animals and humans and to habituate to his environment. Throughout this phase, a good breeder will introduce your puppy to household sounds, smells and contact with a variety of people from an early age.

6 to 16 weeks

This time includes the secondary habituation and

socialization period where the puppy will continue to build social relationships with other dogs, other animals and humans. He will also need to become habituated to as many of the everyday environments he will encounter later as an adult dog. Although he will have a short attention span, it is during this time that your puppy will experience his most rapid learning and what is taught in this period will remain with him for life.

It is therefore the most vital time to introduce a puppy to different environments and people and to make sure that he has plenty of positive experiences. Even though he will not have received his final vaccinations until around 12 weeks, it is still essential that he is taken out to different places. If necessary, carry your puppy in your arms and allow people to handle and make a fuss of him. Introduce him to the sounds of busy roads and every day household noises.

From approximately 8 to 11 weeks, your puppy will also experience his first fear period. During socialization it is important to make sure that he does not suffer any frightening or painful experiences, as puppies of this age generalize their experiences and can become timid and fearful. Should he display any signs of fear or stress during this time, the best thing is to remove him quietly from what is scaring him. Do not make a big fuss as this may reinforce his fears.

From about 10 to 16 weeks, your puppy will begin to work out his place in your household, and he may begin to test his position within the family. It is vital at this time that ground rules have been put in place and all the family is being consistent with instigating them. For example, it is no good one person allowing the puppy on the settee when another person does not. It is said that what is seen at 16 weeks, without any training, is more or less what your dog will be like in his adult life. This is why training at this age is vital so that any unwanted behavior can be prevented.

Towards the end of this period, your puppy will begin losing his baby teeth and mouthing family members can be a problem. Bite inhibition will have been started by the mother and littermates, but this needs to be continued by the rest of the family because you have now replaced his canine family. Never smack your puppy for mouthing, just calmly say either "no" or "ouch" and walk away from him. If he persists, quietly put him in his crate for a few minutes to calm down.

It is important to continue to play with your puppy and handle him on a daily basis, but games like wrestling should be avoided. Tug-of -war games can be played but they should be gentle (as his teeth are changing), and your puppy should be taught that there are rules to the play, such as letting go when asked and being careful not to catch your hands.

Play fighting or wrestling is a game that can rapidly get out of hand. As your puppy's strength grows, he is going to want to play fight to see who is stronger, and even if you win he will learn that this type of play is acceptable which it is not, at any time. He will not know the difference between wrestling with you or a much younger member of the family. Having an adult Rottweiler leaping on someone for a rough and tumble is definitely a no-no.

4 to 8 months

Play instinct period, flight instinct period: It is during this time that your dog could show a reluctance to please you and you may well see him test his limits more and more. It is very important that training and socialization have begun before this time. You need to remain firm, fair and above all consistent in your training methods. The adolescent Rottweiler is no different to the average teenage child and as long as the rules are clear to him, then he will accept them with the minimum fuss. You can avoid problems with chewing by introducing safe chew toys such as kongs and Nylabones for example.

6 to 14 months

From about six months to nine months, the Rottweiler starts to become sexually mature and you may see difference in the behavior of your dog, especially with males who may start to urine mark and mount more frequently. They may also become growly with other male dogs. This is often a stage that they will pass through with correct training and it is important that their socialization continues. Some people suggest ignoring the aggression but it is best that the dogs learn that it is unacceptable with a firm 'no' or 'leave it' command. Increased territoriality can occur, and some dogs can become more assertive when their owners control them. Again, it is very important that socialization and training continues and that household rules remain clear and consistent.

Female dogs generally have their first season between six months to one year of age and changes in scent marking behavior and solicitation of male attention can occur.

The changes in hormones mean that your puppy may experience a second fear Imprint period. This period is where your dog could show fear of something new or even something he is familiar with. If he reacts like this, the best thing is to play the whole situation down. Distract him from the object of his fear as best you can, or even better remove him from it. Again it is important not to fuss and reassure your dog too much as this will only reinforce his anxiety. Positive training during this period usually helps to boost his confidence.

1 to 4 years

Social maturity: Rottweilers are sexually mature by the time they are about one year old, often earlier. However, they continue to mature mentally and physically for some time after this. This period of social maturity brings together the dog's increasing social skills, size and experience. There can be an increase in assertive behavior over other unfamiliar dogs, and also towards people and dogs within their canine and human families, so training must continue into adulthood for this reason. It is vital at this stage that you remain firm but fair with your dog.

Training
guidelines

The Rottweiler, although sometimes strong-willed, is very keen to learn and eager to please. Training will provide hours of pleasure for both you and your puppy. To get the best results, it is important to work out what you want to achieve, and the best way of reaching your goal.

How dogs learn

Dogs learn by a process called conditioning. This means that they come to realize that a particular behavior will produce a consequence, be it positive or negative. Rottweilers respond best to positive consequences. For example, when teaching your Rottweiler to recall in the park, if he receives a big reward for coming back to you, then he is more likely to come every time he is called.

An example of negative training would be to force your dog into a sit position if he will not sit when asked, or to smack him on the nose for mouthing. Negative training or punishment can lead to your Rottweiler becoming aggressive or fearful of you and will not help in building a bond between dog and owner.

Clicker training

This is a highly effective method of positive training, which can be used for all exercises, and for all disciplines. The clicker is a small device that fits in the palm of your hand and makes a sharp clicking noise when pressed and released. The basic concept of clicker training is that the sound marks the correct behavior you are teaching, and the dog learns by the sound that he has done the right thing and can expect a reward.

To begin, your dog must learn that hearing a click will get a reward and the best way to do this is to find a quiet area of your home that your dog is familiar with, and then sit with him and click and feed several times. Repeat this over a few days and he will quickly get the idea. You can test his understanding of this process by clicking and seeing if he reacts to the sound by looking for food.

Giving rewards

Rewarding with treats is a very good way to teach a Rottweiler, as they all love food. When choosing a treat, remember what it is called – a treat. Working for kibble, which your dog gets at mealtimes for free, is hardly worth his while. But if you offer something really tasty, such as cheese, liver or sausage, it will be a different story and you will have a willing pupil on your hands.

The key to successful dog training is making yourself so interesting that your dog will always want to respond to your commands, as he has learned that this produces something that he loves.

Some Rottweilers also like to play, and if you can reward your dog with a satisfying game of tug or ball, this can help strengthen the bond between you.

Below: For some Rottweilers, a game with a toy is a high value reward.

First lessons

It is important, as a family unit, to decide what verbal commands you are going to give to the exercises you teach your Rottweiler, and stick to them. You should only use a command once, in a way that your dog will easily understand. Repeating commands over and over can become confusing for your dog.

Wearing a collar

Make sure that your puppy is used to wearing his collar and lead around the house before taking him out. For the first few times of wearing the collar, he will stop and scratch and it will feel alien to him. If you attach a lead too soon, there is a good chance that he will fight it and his first experience of going out will be marred by having had a negative experience with both the collar and the lead.

Walking on lead

The key to teaching this exercise is patience. Walking your dog should be a pleasurable experience and stress-free. Having an adult Rottweiler towing you to the park is neither, and can also be dangerous.

- Begin training this exercise when your puppy is small by holding a treat or a toy in the hand that he is walking by, and have the lead in the other hand so that it hangs across the front of you.

- Before you set off, make sure you have his attention; using the Watch command (see page 128) works very well here. Then command "Heel" or "Close" and set off. As he is watching you, he will have stayed by your side, so, after a couple of paces, praise and reward. Continue doing this, building up the number of paces in between rewarding.

- As your Rottweiler grows in size, he may well begin to pull on a lead to get to where he wants to go even faster. Remain calm and just stop altogether until he makes eye contact with you – usually when he wants to know why you have stopped!

- When he responds, ask him to come close and start the exercise again. He will soon learn that pulling will not get him where he wants to be any quicker.

Remember to praise and reward when your dog is walking nicely to heel. We are often guilty of nagging when things go wrong and keeping quiet when the dog is responding correctly. He will never learn this way!

Watch me

This command is very useful, as it provides a great way to get your dog's attention. The "Watch me" command focuses your dog on making eye contact with you in a non-threatening way. It is a great command to use if you need to distract your dog at any time.

- Position your dog so that he is sitting in front of you, on a lead if necessary. Have a treat in your hand.

- Bring the treat from your dog's nose to your eyes, and, when he follows the food and his eyes meets yours, click and reward.

- Repeat this process a few times each day before gradually removing the lure of the treat and adding the command "Watch me" as his eyes meets yours.

Teach your Rottweiler the "Watch" command so that he will focus on you, despite distractions.

Socialization

The breeder will have started socializing the puppies, and this is a process you will need to continue intensively for the next 12 months and, indeed, throughout your Rottweiler's life.

To begin with your puppy needs to get used to his home environment and meeting a variety of different people. When he has completed his vaccinations, you can venture into the outside world. Start off in quiet areas and then proceed to busier environments as your Rottweiler gains in confidence.

If your puppy seems anxious, do not pander to him as he will begin to think there really is something to worry about. Encourage him in a calm, business-like manner, and he will learn that there is nothing to be frightened of, and he will learn to cope in a variety of different situations.

It is also important to socialize your Rottweiler with other dogs of sound temperament so that he learns the skills of canine communication. If dogs learn how to read each other body language, it is much easier to avoid conflict. This is particularly important with the Rottweiler, who can be assertive with other dogs.

Facing page:
If you spend time
training and socializing
your Rottweiler, you
will be richly rewarded.

Come when called

This exercise should always be taught in a fun manner with a maximum reward offered at the end. Without a solid recall, you should not let your Rottweiler off his lead in public places.

Begin in the home from the time your puppy comes to live with you.

- Kneel on the floor so you are at your puppy's level and call his name followed by your recall command. Most people use the word "Come" or "Here". It is up to you what command you use as long as you stick to the same one. You can also clap your hands at this time to make yourself more exciting.

- Your puppy will run happily towards you, and, as soon as he gets to you, give him his reward, whether it is food or a game.

- Move this training to the garden and practise calling him and making a big fuss when he comes. He may become distracted in the garden, with its different smells, so be patient and persevere with making yourself even more exciting.

When you start taking your Rottweiler out to the local park, it is best to use a training line, which is a lightweight line considerably longer than a normal lead. They come in varying lengths; a line of around 10 to 15 feet (3-4.5 m) is ideal for recall training, as it prevents your dog from failing.

- Attach the training line to your dog's collar and allow him to wander off.

- After a short time, call him as you would have done in the garden. If he comes running to you then reward as before and immediately let him go again. In this way, he also learns that being recalled in the park does not mean the end of a walk.

- Get into the practice of talking hold of your Rottweiler's collar as he comes back and is rewarded, so that he never gets collar shy. Your dog will quickly learn that you only hold his collar to put him back on a lead at the end of a walk. He therefore begins to jump away as you reach down to him. By always taking hold of his collar when recalling him – and then letting him go again – we can prevent this behavior forming.

- If your Rottweiler ignores you when you have called him, simply pick up the training line to prevent him going out of range and this should attract his attention. Call him again, making yourself as exciting as possible, and reward when he gets back to you.

By following this training method, as your Rottweiler goes through his different learning stages, you can keep him from going wrong and, when regularly reinforced, the behavior you want will remain with him for life.

Your Rottweiler must think it is the best fun in the world to return to your side.

Stationary exercises

These are easy to teach, and they can be used in many different situations, giving you good control over your dog.

Sit

- Take a treat and hold it towards your puppy's nose. Slowly raise the treat upwards and slightly heading back over his head.

- As your puppy lifts his head to watch the treat, his bottom will naturally hit the floor and you can click and reward.

- Once he is doing this every time, you can begin to add the command "Sit" just as the puppy goes into position.

Never push down on your Rottweiler's bottom, as this could damage his hips or joints, and, by placing him into position, he will never learn for himself.

It is like teaching a child to tie his shoelaces: if you always tie them for him, then he will never learn how to do it.

Down

This is probably one of the most important exercises that you can teach your Rottweiler. A reliable instant down could one day save his life if he is running towards a road.

- Hold a treat in your hand and place it, palm-down, on the floor and wait.

- Your puppy will put his nose to your hand to smell the treat. Eventually, he will flop down to continue sniffing. As soon as he does, click and lift your hand to uncover the treat.

- As with the Sit exercise, once he is going down regularly then begin to add the "Down" command when he is in the correct position.

- Once he has learned the word, you then need to begin to remove the hand signal.

This exercise can be progressed by teaching instant downs, which is done by throwing a treat for your dog and, when he has run to it and eaten it, command him to "Down" and click and reward when he does it. This needs to be kept fun and light-hearted and your puppy will learn, seeing it as a game.

An instant response to the "Down" command can be a lifesaver.

Control exercises

These exercises may not seen the most exciting, but they have two-fold value. You are establishing control over your dog, which is important in a breed as big and powerful as the Rottweiler, and it teaches him to respect you. He must learn to inhibit his natural, exuberant behavior and do as you ask.

Stay

Once you have a reliable Sit or Down, you can begin to teach the Stay command.

- Ask your puppy to "Sit" or go "Down" and then count out loud to five. Your puppy should stay as you have left him, as the sound of your counting will distract him from moving.

- Once you have got to five then click and reward.

- Continue with this, and then progress by increasing your count to 10 and then 15 and so on. At this stage, introduce the "Stay" command before you start counting.

- Once you can count to 30, go back to counting to 10, but only count every other number out loud – i.e. one, three, five and gradually build this up to 30.

- Continue using this method of reducing the numbers you say out loud until you can just give the "Stay" command.

The next step is to start increasing distance.

- Ask your puppy to "Sit" or go "Down" and command him to "Stay". Then begin to count out loud and, at the same time, take a pace or two away from him and then go straight back.

- As with the first part of the exercise, you can gradually build up distance by using the counting method.

If, at any time, your puppy breaks his Stay, do not get cross with him; simply place him back in his Stay position and start again. Never be afraid to go back a few stages to really cement his knowledge. Basic training is the foundation, and, as with buildings, a strong foundation will last.

Once you start to leave your dog in the Stay, always stand sideways on to him, to avoid him thinking that you are going to recall him, and do not offer him any eye contact. Keep the training to short periods to avoid your dog becoming bored and distracted.

Leave it!

This is a universal command and can be used not only to ask your dog to leave something that may have been dropped on the floor, but also to stop any unwanted interaction with another dog.

- Make sure you have a high-level reward (such as a piece of sausage) in your hand and a bowl with something less desirable (such as a dog biscuit).

- Put your puppy on a lead to prevent him from getting to the biscuit.

- Place the bowl close to your puppy, and, as he goes towards it, say, "Leave it" in a strong, low voice. This should initially startle your puppy into looking at you.

- As soon as your Rottweiler looks at you, click and reward him with the high-level reward.

- Repeat this, using the lead to prevent the puppy from getting to the bowl. Never correct on the lead, as this is not necessary. He will quickly learn that "Leave it" means 'give eye contact and a tasty reward will follow'.

It is very important that your puppy never gets what you are asking him to leave. So if you have asked him to leave a biscuit, do not feed him that biscuit but take another out.

Many people teach this command as a Wait before allowing the dog to eat at mealtimes.

However, "Leave it" should be permanent, as you do not want your dog to leave something harmful for a short period of time only. Once a dog hears this command, he should understand that it means forever.

This is a good command to use when your Rottweiler reaches adolescence. Should he become aggressive towards other dogs, a firm "Leave it" from the beginning will demonstrate that he cannot act in this manner. Always remember to reward highly when he does respond.

Opportunities for Rottweilers

Once you have completed basic training, you may like to move on to more advanced training and have a go at competing in one of the dog sports.

Good Citizen Scheme

The Kennel Club Good Citizen Scheme was introduced to promote responsible dog ownership, and to teach dogs basic good manners. In the US there is one test; in the UK there are four award levels: Puppy Foundation, Bronze, Silver and Gold.

Exercises within the scheme include:

• Walking on lead

• Road walking

• Control at door/gate

• Food manners

- Recall

- Stay

- Send to bed

- Emergency stop

Competitive obedience

This is a sport where you are assessed as a dog and handler, completing a series of exercises including heelwork, recalls, retrieves, stays, sendaways and scent discrimination.

The exercises are relatively simple to begin with, involving heelwork, a recall and stays in the lowest class. As you progress, more exercises are added, and the aids you are allowed to give are reduced.

To achieve top honours in this discipline, requires intensive training, as precision and accuracy are of paramount importance.

Tracking

The versatile Rottweiler is a good choice for this demanding sport where the dog must learn to follow scent trails of varying age, over different types of terrain. In the US, this is a sport in its own right; in the UK it is incorporated into Working Trials where a dog must also compete in two other elements – control and agility.

Agility

In this sport, the dog completes an obstacle course under the guidance of his owner. You need a good element of control, as the dog completes the course off the lead. In competition, each dog completes the course individually and is assessed on both time and accuracy. The dog who completes the course with the fewest faults in the fastest time, wins the class. The obstacles include an A-frame, a dog-walk, weaving poles, a seesaw, tunnels, and jumps.

Showing

In this discipline, a dog is assessed by a judge on his conformation, movement and temperament, according to the stipulations of the Breed Standard.

Your puppy will need training in ringcraft from a young age, as he will be looked over by the judge and will need to learn to stand patiently for long periods of time. He will also need to be able to move at a fast pace with his handler and remain under control while doing so.

There are different classes, depending on the age of your dog, and the dream is make your Rottweiler into a Show Champion.

A lean, fit Rottweiler will make his mark in agility.

The ideal owner

The Rottweiler is a powerful, intelligent dog with a mind of his own. Things go wrong when people take on this breed without sufficient knowledge or experience. The ideal owner should:

- Work out a comprehensive programme of socialization, giving their dog the opportunity to meet people of all ages, to interact with other dogs of sound temperament, and to be exposed to a wide variety of different situations.

- Allocate time for basic training and then find an outlet for the Rottweiler's mental energies. Ideally, this would entail further training in one of the canine sports, but it could be something as simple as teaching your dog tricks to do at home.

- Be firm but fair, and remain consistent in all dealings with your Rottweiler, so that he understands his place in the family unit.

Sony Xperia E3

Health care

Health care

We are fortunate that the Rottweiler is a healthy dog, with no exaggerations, and with good routine care, a well-balanced diet, and sufficient exercise, most dogs will experience few health problems.

However, it is your responsibility to put a programme of preventative health care in place – and this should start from the moment your puppy, or older dog, arrives in his new home.

Vaccinations

Dogs are subject to a number of contagious diseases. In the old days, these were killers, and resulted in heartbreak for many owners. Vaccinations have now been developed, and the occurrence of the major infectious diseases is now very rare. However, this will only remain the case if all pet owners follow a strict policy of vaccinating their dogs.

Vaccinations are available for the following diseases:

Adenovirus: This affects the liver; affected dogs have a classic 'blue eye'.

Distemper: A viral disease, which causes chest and gastro-intestinal damage. The brain may also be affected, leading to fits and paralysis.

Parvovirus: Causes severe gastro enteritis, and most commonly affects puppies.

Leptospirosis: This bacterial disease is carried by rats and affects many mammals, including humans. It causes liver and kidney damage.

Rabies: A virus that affects the nervous system and is invariably fatal. The first signs are abnormal behavior when the infected dog may bite another animal or a person. Paralysis and death follow. Vaccination is compulsory in most countries. In the UK, dogs travelling overseas must be vaccinated.

Kennel Cough: There are several strains of kennel cough, but they all result in a harsh, dry, cough. This disease is rarely fatal; in fact most dogs make a good recovery within a matter of weeks and show few signs of ill health while they are affected. However, kennel cough is highly infectious among dogs that live together so, for this reason, most boarding kennels will insist that your dog is protected by the vaccine, which is given as nose drops.

Lyme Disease: This is a bacterial disease transmitted by ticks (see page 164). The first signs are limping, but the heart, kidneys and nervous system can also be affected. The ticks that transmit the disease occur in specific regions, such as the north-east states of the USA, some of the southern states, California and the upper Mississippi region. Lyme disease is till rare in the UK so vaccinations are not routinely offered.

Vaccination programme

In the USA, the American Animal Hospital Association advises vaccination for core diseases, which they list as: distemper, adenovirus, parvovirus and rabies. The requirement for vaccinating for non-core diseases – leptospirosis, lyme disease and kennel cough – should be assessed depending on a dog's individual risk and his likely exposure to the disease.

In the UK, vaccinations are routinely given for distemper, adenovirus, leptospirosis and parvovirus.

Facing page:
You will need to
continue the worming
programme started by
your puppy's breeder.

In most cases, a puppy will start his vaccinations at around eight weeks of age, with the second part given in a fortnight's time. However, this does vary depending on the individual policy of veterinary practices, and the incidence of disease in your area.

You should also talk to your vet about whether to give annual booster vaccinations. This depends on an individual dog's levels of immunity, and how long a particular vaccine remains effective.

Parasites

No matter how well you look after your Rottweiler, you will have to accept that parasites – internal and external – are ever present, and you need to take preventative action.

Internal parasites: As the name suggests, these parasites live inside your dog. Most will find a home in the digestive tract, but there is also a parasite that lives in the heart. If infestation is unchecked, a dog's health will be severely jeopardized, but routine preventative treatment is simple and effective.

External parasites: These parasites live on your dog's body – on his skin and fur, and sometimes in his ears.

Roundworm

This is found in the small intestine, and signs of infestation will be a poor coat, a pot belly, diarrhoea and lethargy. Pregnant mothers should be treated, but it is almost inevitable that parasites will be passed on to the puppies. For this reason, a breeder will start a worming programme, which you will need to continue. Ask your vet for advice on treatment, which will need to continue throughout your dog's life.

Tapeworm

Infection occurs when fleas and lice are ingested. The adult worm takes up residence in the small intestine, releasing mobile segments (which contain eggs) which can be seen in a dog's feces as small rice-like grains. The only other obvious sign of infestation is irritation of the anus. Again, routine preventative treatment is required throughout your Rottweiler's life.

Heartworm

This parasite is transmitted by mosquitoes, and so it is more likely to be present in warm, humid climates. However, it is found in all parts of the USA, although its prevalence does vary. At present, heartworm is rarely seen in the UK.

Heartworms live in the right side of the heart and larvae can grow up to 14 in (35 cm) in length. A dog with heartworm is at severe risk from heart failure, so preventative treatment, as advised by your vet, is essential. Dogs living in the USA should also have regular tests to check for infection.

Lungworm

Lungworm, or *Angiostrongylus vasorum*, is a parasite that lives in the heart and major blood vessels supplying the lungs. It can cause many problems, such as breathing difficulties, excessive bleeding, sickness and diarrhoea, seizures, and can even be fatal. The parasite is carried by slugs and snails, and the dog becomes infected when ingesting these, often accidentally when rummaging through undergrowth. Lungworm is not common, but it is on the increase and a responsible owner should be aware of it. Fortunately, it is easily preventable and even affected dogs usually make a full recovery if treated early enough. Your vet will be able to advise you on the risk in your area and what form of treatment may be required.

Fleas

A dog may carry dog fleas, cat fleas, and even human fleas. The flea stays on the dog only long enough to feed and breed, but its presence will result in itching.

If your dog has an allergy to fleas – usually a reaction to the flea's saliva – he will scratch himself until raw.

Spot-on treatment, administered on a routine basis, is easy to use and highly effective on all types of fleas. You can also treat your dog with a spray or with insecticidal shampoo. Bear in mind that the whole environment your dog lives in will need to be sprayed, and all other pets living in your home will also need to be treated.

How to detect fleas

You may suspect your dog has fleas, but how can you be sure? There are two methods to try.

Run a fine comb through your dog's coat, and see if you can detect the presence of fleas on the skin, or clinging to the comb. Alternatively, sit your dog on white paper and rub his back. This will dislodge feces from the fleas, which will be visible as small brown specks. To double check, shake the specks on to some damp cotton wool (cotton). Flea feces consists of the dried blood taken from the host, so if the specks turn a lighter shade of red, you know your dog has fleas.

Ticks

These are most frequently found in rural area where sheep or deer are present. The main danger is their ability to pass Lyme disease to both dogs and humans. Lyme disease is prevalent in some areas of the USA (see page 156), although it is still rare in the UK. The treatment you give your dog for fleas generally works for ticks, but you should discuss the best product to use with your vet.

How to remove a tick

If you spot a tick on your dog, do not try to pluck it off as you risk leaving the hard mouth parts embedded in his skin. The best way to remove a tick is to use a fine pair of tweezers or you can buy a tick remover. Grasp the tick head firmly and then pull the tick straight out from the skin. If you are using a tick remover, check the instructions, as some recommend a circular twist when pulling. When you have removed the tick, clean the area with mild soap and water.

Ear mites

These parasites live in the outer ear canal. The signs of infestation are a brown, waxy discharge, and your dog will continually shake his head and scratch his ear. If you suspect your Rottweiler has ear mites, visit your vet, as he will probably need to prescribe treatment.

Fur mites

These small, white parasites are visible to the naked eye and are often referred to as 'walking dandruff'. They cause a scurfy coat and mild itchiness. However, they are zoonotic – transferable to humans – so prompt treatment with an insecticide prescribed by your vet is essential.

Harvest mites

These are picked up from the undergrowth, and can be seen as a bright orange patch on the webbing between the toes, although this can be found elsewhere on the body, such as on the ear flaps. Treatment is effective with the appropriate insecticide.

Skin mites

There are two types of parasite that burrow into a dog's skin. Demodex canis is transferred from a mother to her pups while they are feeding. Treatment is with a topical preparation, and sometimes antibiotics are needed.

The other skin mite is sarcoptes scabiei, which causes intense itching and hair loss. It is highly contagious, so all dogs in a household will need to be treated, which involves repeated bathing with a medicated shampoo.

Common
ailments

As with all living animals, dogs can be affected by a variety of ailments, most of which can be treated effectively after consulting with your vet, who will prescribe appropriate medication and will advise you on how to care for your dog's needs. Here are some of the more common problems that could affect your Rottweiler, with advice on how to deal with them.

Anal glands

These are two small sacs on either side of the anus, which produce a dark-brown secretion that dogs use when they mark their territory. The anal glands should empty every time a dog defecates but, if they become blocked or impacted, a dog will experience increasing discomfort. He may nibble at his rear end,

or 'scoot' his bottom along the ground to relieve the irritation. Treatment involves a trip to the vet, who will empty the glands manually. It is important to do this without delay or infection may occur.

Dental problems

Good dental hygiene will do much to minimize problems with gum infection and tooth decay. If tartar accumulates to the extent that you cannot remove it by brushing, the vet will need to intervene. In a situation such as this, an anesthetic will need to be administered so the tartar can be removed manually.

Diarrhoea

There are many reasons why a dog has diarrhoea, but most commonly it is the result of scavenging, a sudden change of diet, or an adverse reaction to a particular type of food.

If your dog is suffering from diarrhoea, first withdraw food for a day. It is important that he does not dehydrate, so make sure that fresh drinking water is available. However, drinking too much can increase the diarrhoea, which may be accompanied by vomiting, so limit how much he drinks at any one time.

After allowing the stomach to rest, feed a bland diet, such as white fish or chicken with boiled rice for a few days. In most cases, your dog's motions will return to normal and you can resume normal feeding, although this should be done gradually.

However, if this fails to work and the diarrhoea persists for more than a few days, you should consult you vet. Your dog may have an infection, which needs to be treated with antibiotics, or the diarrhoea may indicate some other problem which needs expert diagnosis.

Ear infections

The Rottweiler's ears lie close to his head so air cannot circulate as freely as it would in a dog with semi-pricked or pricked ears. Therefore, it is important to keep a close check on your Rottweiler's ears.

A healthy ear is clean with no sign of redness or inflammation, and no evidence of a waxy brown discharge or a foul odor. If you see your dog scratching his ear, shaking his head, or holding one ear at an odd angle, you will need to consult your vet.

The most likely causes are ear mites, an infection, or there may a foreign body, such as a grass seed, trapped in the ear.

Depending on the cause, treatment is with medicated ear drops, possibly containing antibiotics. If a foreign body is suspected, the vet will need to carry our further investigations.

Eye problems

The Rottweiler's eyes are set square in his skull; they do not protrude, as in breeds such as the Pug, so they are less vulnerable to injury.

However, if your Rottweiler's eyes look red and sore, he may be suffering from Conjunctivitis. This may be accompanied by a watery or crusty discharge. Conjunctivitis can be caused by a bacterial or viral infection. It could be the result of an injury, or it could be an adverse reaction to pollen.

You will need to consult your vet for a correct diagnosis, but in the case of an infection, treatment with medicated eye drops is effective.

Conjunctivitis may also be the first sign of more serious inherited eye problems (see page 182).

A Rottweiler's eyes should be bright and sparkling, with no hint of soreness or discharge.

Sore and inflamed eyes may also be the result of a foreign body, such as a grass seed, entering the eye (see below).

Foreign bodies

In the home, puppies – and some older dogs – cannot resist chewing anything that looks interesting. Even when he is only a puppy, a Rottweiler has powerful jaws, and when he has his adult teeth, he can be very destructive.

The toys you choose for your dog should be suitably robust to withstand damage, but children's toys can be irresistible. Some dogs will chew – and swallow – anything from socks, tights, and other items from the laundry basket, to golf balls and stones from the garden. Obviously, these items are indigestible and could cause an obstruction in your dog's intestine, which is potentially lethal.

The signs to look for are vomiting, and a tucked up posture. The dog will often be restless and will look as though he is in pain.

The other type of foreign body that may cause problems is grass seed. A grass seed can enter an orifice such as a nostril, down an ear, the gap between the eye and the eyelid, or penetrate the soft skin between the toes. It can also be swallowed.

The introduction of a foreign body induces a variety of symptoms, depending on the point of entry and where it travels to. The signs to look for include head shaking/ear scratching, the eruption of an abscess, sore, inflamed eyes, or a persistent cough. The vet will be able to make a proper diagnosis, and surgery may be required.

As a preventative measure, avoid exercising your Rottweiler in areas of long grass when it is seeding, and if he strays into grassland, groom him and examine him thoroughly when you return home.

Heatstroke

The Rottweiler is a heavyweight breed, and he has a tendency to overheat. When the temperature rises, make sure your dog always has access to shady areas, and wait for a cooler part of the day before going for a walk. Be extra careful if you leave your Rottweiler in the car, as the temperature can rise dramatically even on a cloudy day. Heatstroke can happen very rapidly, and unless you are able lower your dog's temperature, it can be fatal.

If your Rottweiler appears to be suffering from heatstroke, lie him flat and then cool him as quickly as possible by hosing him, covering him with wet towels, or using frozen food bags from the freezer. As soon as he has made some recovery, take him to the vet where cold intravenous fluids can be administered.

Lameness/Limping

There are a wide variety of reasons why a dog can go lame, from a simple muscle strain to a fracture, ligament damage, or more complex problems with the joints which may be an inherited disorder (see pages 184). It takes an expert to make a correct diagnosis, so if you are concerned about your dog, do not delay in seeking help.

As your Rottweiler becomes elderly, he may suffer from arthritis, which you will see as general stiffness, particularly when he gets up after resting. It will help if you ensure his bed is in a warm, draught-free location, and, if your Rottweiler gets wet after exercise, you must dry him thoroughly.

If your elderly Rottweiler seems to be in pain, consult your vet who will be able to help with pain relief medication.

The heavily-built Rottweiler is prone to suffer in the heat, so take extra care on hot days.

Lumps

As your Rottweiler gets older, you may notice a lump appearing on his body. These are usually benign, but there is a possibility that it could be malignant. Regardless of your Rottweiler's age, any lumps that you notice should be examined by your vet, who may advise taking a sample to be checked by a pathologist to determine treatment.

Skin problems

If your dog is scratching or nibbling at his skin, the first thing to check for is fleas. There are other external parasites, such as skin mites, which cause itching and hair loss, but you will need a vet to help you find the culprit.

Acute moist dermatitis, also known as hot spot, may occur when a dog keeps scratching an area and the skins becomes wet and infected. A course of antibiotic treatment will be required.

Rolling may indicate an itchy skin although this Rottweiler is simply enjoying a roll in the sand.

An allergic reaction is another major cause of skin problems, resulting in a condition known as Atopy. It can be quite an undertaking to find the cause of the allergy, and you will need to follow your vet's advice, which often requires eliminating specific ingredients from the diet, as well as looking at environmental factors.

Inherited disorders

The Rottweiler does have a few breed-related disorders, and if diagnosed with any of the diseases listed here, it is important to remember that they can affect offspring, so breeding from affected dogs should be discouraged.

There are now recognized screening tests to enable breeders to check for affected individuals and hence reduce the prevalence of these diseases within the breed.

For details of the organizations concerned, see pages 182 and 185.

DNA testing is also becoming more widely available, and as research into the different genetic diseases progresses, more DNA tests are being developed.

Aortic Stenosis (AS)

This is a malformation of the aortic valve in the heart, and is present at birth. Narrowing of the valve causes the blood to be pushed through the heart at a faster velocity than normal. This increased effort results in an increase in size of the left ventricle muscle of the heart, as the muscle works harder.

Rottweilers with mild forms of AS can show no clinical signs. More severe forms are usually degenerative and heart failure will occur as the heart loses the ability to cope. Restricted exercise may help slow the progression of the disease and medications can be prescribed to help the heart. Affected dogs should not be bred from.

Bloat

Also known as gastric dilatation, the stomach swells visibly, and then rotates, so that the exit into the small intestine becomes blocked, preventing food from leaving. This results in stomach pain and a bloated abdomen. It is a severe, life-threatening condition that requires immediate veterinary attention (usually surgery) to decompress the stomach and return it to its normal position.

Rottweilers may be at risk, as it is usually seen in large deep-chested breeds. Greedy, fast-eating

Strenuous exercise should be avoided before and after mealtimes.

dogs may be more susceptible, and this is further compounded by exercise immediately before or after eating. It is advisable to adopt a regime where you do not exercise your Rottweiler an hour before feeding, and wait for two hours after feeding before allowing exercise.

If your Rottweiler has a tendency to bolt his food, you can buy a special bowl, which is designed to make a dog eat more slowly. These are available in most pet stores.

Canine acne

Rottweilers may be affected by thus condition, which is also known as muzzle furunculosis. It is similar to acne in humans and appears as blackheads on the muzzle which can progress to pustules and infected spots. Treatment is in the form of shampoos or antibiotics.

Eye disorders

There are two eye conditions which most commonly affect Rottweilers – entropion and ectropion. Testing is carried out by the Canine Eye Registration Foundation in the US; in the UK there is a combined scheme run by the British Veterinary Association, the Kennel Club and the International Sheep Dog Society.

Entropion is an inrolling of the eyelids, which may result in inflammation and infection. Small, wart-like growths on the lids may occur, which is not usually a problem unless they grow large or touch the cornea, causing trauma. More severe cases of entropion may require surgery.

Ectropion occurs when the eyelids roll outwards. This is a condition which often improves with age, and surgery is rarely required.

Joint disorders

The Rottweiler is a large, fast-growing breed and, as a result, he is vulnerable to joint problems, particularly during the growing period. These may include:

Cruciate rupture

The cruciate ligaments of the stifle (knee) can be partially or completely torn when placed under high amounts of physical stress, resulting in lameness. This condition is relatively common in Rottweilers, especially if overweight, which applies unnecessary stress on the ligaments. Treatment often involves surgery along with an extended period of rest and the affected joint is prone to arthritis later in life.

Elbow dysplasia (ED)

This is a developmental disease where the elbow does not mature correctly and signs of lameness are usually seen in younger, large-breed dogs. There appears to be an increased incidence of ED in Rottweilers, so it is essential that all breeding stock is tested.

In the US, X-rays are submitted to the Orthopedic Foundation for Animals; in the UK X-rays are sent to the British Veterinary Association where a panel will give a grading to each elbow. Severely affected dogs should not be used for breeding.

Surgery may be indicated to correct the abnormalities, but the affected joints will be more prone to arthritis later in life.

Hip dysplasia (HD)

This is where the ball-and-socket joint of the hip develops incorrectly so that the head of the femur (ball) and the acetabulum of the pelvis (socket) do not fit snugly. This causes pain in the joint and may be seen as lameness in dogs as young as five months old with deterioration into severe arthritis over time.

In the US, hip scoring is carried out by the Orthopedic Foundation for Animals. X-rays are submitted when a dog is two years old, categorized as Normal (Excellent, Good, Fair), Borderline, and Dysplastic (Mild, Moderate, Severe). The hip grades of Excellent, Good and Fair are within normal limits and are given OFA numbers.

In the UK, the minimum age for the hips to be assessed by X-ray is 12 months.   Each hip can score from a possible perfect 0 to a deformed 53. Both left and right scores are added together to give the total hip score.

Careful and responsible breeding over the years has reduced the prevalence of this disease in Rottweilers, but care must be taken to ensure that this continues into the future.

Osteochondrosis and osteochondritis dissecans (OCD)

This is where there is inflammation and pain of the bone and cartilage, often due to abnormalities or trauma, and the ensuing damage resulting in a flap of cartilage breaking off into the joint (joint mouse). Occasionally seen in the younger, growing Rottweiler, this can be a very painful condition, especially if the fragment moves within the joint, and surgery may be needed to remove it.

Panosteitis

Inflammation of the long bones of the legs can occur in young, large/giant breed dogs. This causes clinical signs of lameness without an initiating cause that may alternate between all four legs (shifting lameness). Pain levels vary from mild to severe. If mild, most dogs are back to normal by two years of age, but if severe then anti-inflammatories and restricted exercise will be required.

Osteosarcoma

This is a bone tumor that affects Rottweilers, commonly found in the long bones of the legs (but may also be found elsewhere in the skeleton). Initial clinical signs are lameness, swelling and pain, but may progress to fracture in more severe cases.

Treatment to improve survival times may include surgery, chemotherapy or radiotherapy.

Summing up

It may give the pet owner cause for concern to find about health problems that may affect their dog. But it is important to bear in mind that acquiring some basic knowledge is an asset, as it will allow you to spot signs of trouble at an early stage. Early diagnosis is very often the means to the most effective treatment.

Fortunately, the Rottweiler is a generally healthy and disease-free dog with his only visits to the vet being annual check-ups. In most cases, owners can look forward to enjoying many happy years with this loyal family protector.

Useful addresses

Breed Kennel Clubs

Please contact your Kennel Club to obtain contact information about breed clubs in your area.

UK

The Kennel Club (UK)
1 Clarges Street London, W1J 8AB
Telephone: 0870 606 6750
Fax: 0207 518 1058
Web: www.thekennelclub.org.uk

USA

American Kennel Club (AKC)
5580 Centerview Drive, Raleigh, NC 27606.
Telephone: 919 233 9767
Fax: 919 233 3627
Email: info@akc.org
Web: www.akc.org

United Kennel Club (UKC)
100 E Kilgore Rd, Kalamazoo,
MI 49002-5584, USA.
Tel: 269 343 9020
Fax: 269 343 7037
Web: www.ukcdogs.com

Australia

Australian National Kennel Council (ANKC)
The Australian National Kennel Council is the administrative body for pure breed canine affairs in Australia. It does not, however, deal directly with dog exhibitors, breeders or judges. For information pertaining to breeders, clubs or shows, please contact the relevant State or Territory Body.

International

Fédération Cynologique Internationalé (FCI)
Place Albert 1er, 13, B-6530 Thuin, Belgium.
Tel: +32 71 59.12.38
Fax: +32 71 59.22.29
Web: www.fci.be

Training and behavior

UK

Association of Pet Dog Trainers
Telephone: 01285 810811
Web: www.apdt.co.uk

Association of Pet Behaviour Counsellors
Telephone: 01386 751151
Web: www.apbc.org.uk

USA

Association of Pet Dog Trainers
Tel: 1 800 738 3647
Web: www.apdt.com

American College of Veterinary Behaviorists
Web: www.dacvb.org

American Veterinary Society of Animal Behavior
Web: www.avsabonline.org

Australia

APDT Australia Inc
Web: www.apdt.com.au

Canine Behavior
For details of regional behvaiourists, contact the relevant State or Territory Controlling Body.

Agility Club
Web: www.agilityclub.co.uk

British Flyball Association
Telephone: 01628 829623
Web: www.flyball.org.uk

North American Dog Agility Council
Web: www.nadac.com

North American Flyball Association, Inc.
Tel/Fax: 800 318 6312
Web: www.flyball.org

Agility Dog Association of Australia
Tel: 0423 138 914
Web: www.adaa.com.au

NADAC Australia
Web: www.nadacaustralia.com

Australian Flyball Association
Tel: 0407 337 939
Web: www.flyball.org.au

World Canine Freestyle Organisation
Tel: (718) 332-8336
Web: www.worldcaninefreestyle.org

British Small Animal Veterinary Association
Tel: 01452 726700
Web: www.bsava.com

Royal College of Veterinary Surgeons
Tel: 0207 222 2001
Web: www.rcvs.org.uk

www.dogbooksonline.co.uk/healthcare

Alternative Veterinary Medicine Centre
Tel: 01367 710324
Web: www.alternativevet.org

American Veterinary Medical Association
Tel: 800 248 2862
Web: www.avma.org

American College of Veterinary Surgeons
Tel: 301 916 0200
Toll Free: 877 217 2287
Web: www.acvs.org

Canine Eye Registration Foundation
The Veterinary Medical DataBases
1717 Philo Rd, PO Box 3007,
Urbana, IL 61803-3007
Tel: 217-693-4800
Fax: 217-693-4801
Web: www.vmdb.org/cerf.html

Orthopaedic Foundation of Animals
2300 E Nifong Boulevard
Columbia, Missouri, 65201-3806
Tel: 573 442-0418
Fax: 573 875-5073
Web: www.offa.org

American Holistic Veterinary Medical
Association
Tel: 410 569 0795
Web: www.ahvma.org

Australian Small Animal Veterinary
Association
Tel: 02 9431 5090
Web: www.asava.com.au

Australian Veterinary Association
Tel: 02 9431 5000
Web: www.ava.com.au

Australian College Veterinary Scientists
Tel: 07 3423 2016
Web: www.acvsc.org.au

Australian Holistic Vets
Web: www.ahv.com.au